breathe life
INTO YOUR
dreams

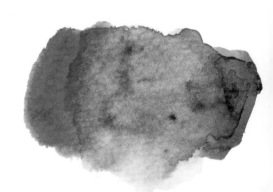

IMAGINE
Out Loud
A Journal of Creative Discovery

with

jane davenport

Get Creative 6

Get Creative 6
An imprint of Mixed Media Resources
104 West 27th Street
New York, NY 10001
Connect with us on Facebook at facebook.com/getcreative6

ISBN: 978-1-64021-049-3
Manufactured in China

1 3 5 7 9 10 8 6 4 2

First Edition

believe
and
sparkle

Introduction

Hello, lovely! I'm so excited you picked up this journal. Journals—both diaries and art journals—have always been my constant companions, a place of refuge and a safe space to nurture my dreams and creativity.

Journaling has so many benefits. Writing down your thoughts is very calming and helps put things in perspective. Are you like me? Do you have thoughts swirling in your head? Ideas, worries, inspiration? The best way to wrangle these thoughts is to write them down! If you put them down on paper, you don't have to keep them in your head. Journals are a wonderful place to ideate and let your dreams take shape.

Modern life often leaves us feeling pulled in different directions. Yes, we have more opportunity, but overload can lead to stress, which makes journaling a wonderful way to prioritize a bit of self-care. A little time away from other areas of your life—your work, your family, your home—allows you to creatively reset and make space in your life. Take some time for yourself, guilt free!

I really treat my journals like a lab to experiment in, so anything goes!

A blank page can seem intimidating. You may ask, "Where do I start?" or fear you're going to "mess up." The beauty of this journal is that it's full of prompts and art that will give you that nudge and focus to get started. The prompts are open-ended to allow for your interpretation. I've also included quotations—both my own "Jane-isms" and others from people I admire—along with colorful artwork to further inspire you.

The prompts are intended to spur your creativity, whether that's through writing, drawing, painting, or all of the above! Creativity is about looking at things a little differently, at taking a different approach to a problem, about manifesting the life you dream of. Everyone can do with a little more creativity in their lives.

Take time for yourself. Slow down. Try journaling in a favorite quiet place, in a café, or on your commute. Step into the journal and let your mind relax and play. Remember: It's your journal. Write, doodle, dream, *imagine!*

jane davenport

shine

Light

Think about how you can be a source of light to other people.

Live with
one foot in
a fairy tale

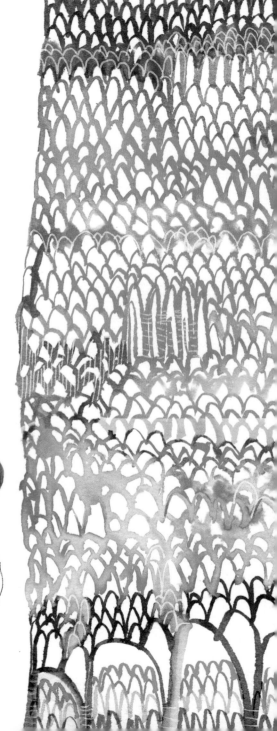

Write a fairy tale in which you are the heroine.
Update a classic or create your own.

What inspires you? Travel? Books? Other people?
What are some ways you can feel more inspired every day?

A FEW OF
my favourite
things

If you had to leave your home for good in a hurry, which five possessions would you take with you? Why are they so important?

your heart
is your
greatest
treasure.

What is closest to your heart? A person? A cause? A passion?

Describe or draw your ideal garden regardless of climate, the greenness of your thumbs, or the size of your home. Is it a tropical paradise, a peaceful Zen garden, a cottage garden bursting with roses?

The world lies in the hands of those who have the courage to dream and who take the risk of living out their dreams—each according to his or her **talent**.

What are three dreams you would pursue if you had a 100-percent chance of succeeding? What are three dreams you would follow even if you knew they would probably fail?

breathe life
INTO YOUR
dreams
WITH YOUR
creativity

Draw a picture or write a story in which you're living a dream. Describe it in detail.

Invent ten new words that describe you.

_____

_____

_____

_____

_____

_____

_____

_____

_____

_____

Do you have fears that are holding you back?
Where do you think they come from?
Are they real?

the moment we
set off in search of
our 'style'
it sets off in search
of us.

Circle the words that describe your style — your personal style, your home, your art. Are there any other ways you'd describe your style?

funky	tranquil	cozy
flamboyant	unconventional	retro
colorful	tasteful	sporty
edgy	flashy	chic
boho	glittering	glamorous
sophisticated	natural	whimsical
demure	mysterious	exotic
minimalist	enigmatic	dramatic
contemporary	abstract	elegant
clean	flowery	sexy
bold	ethereal	playful
rocker	poetic	down-to-earth
punk	timeless	crafty
vintage	monochromatic	feminine
relaxed	rustic	_____
dreamy	sunny	_____
romantic	classic	_____
organic	eclectic	_____
graceful	global	_____
delicate	cheerful	_____

xoxo

FACE YOUR PROBLEMS.
You will discover
that you are
FAR MORE CAPABLE
than you thought.

Write down three to five things that are troubling you.
What small steps can you take to start solving these problems?

THE Artist has the Universe in their MIND & HANDS

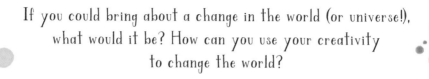

If you could bring about a change in the world (or universe!), what would it be? How can you use your creativity to change the world?

Write a letter to your younger self. Knowing what you know now, what advice would you give to help her realize her potential?

Design your ideal creative space no matter what your creative outlet is. Describe it or draw a floor plan.

oh! How
DELIGHTFUL!

Write about a few things that made you smile this week—a
beautiful view, seeing a favorite person, a funny joke . . .

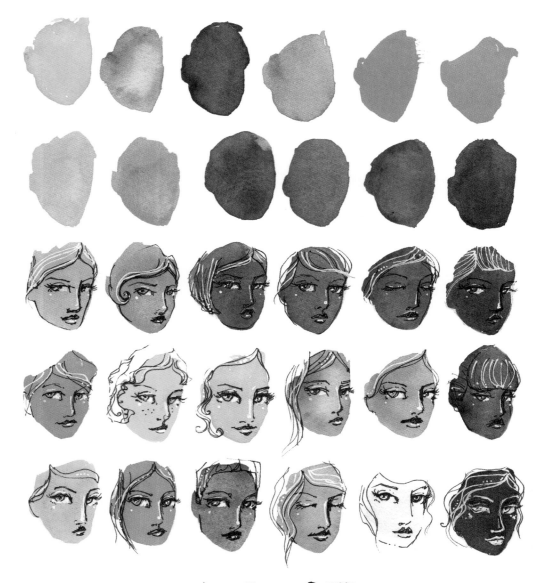

EMBRACE
the PROCESS

What do you find you "lose yourself" doing?
Cooking, painting, gardening, decorating, making lists?
How do you feel when you're in the moment?

you don't
need to feed
your INNER CRITIC

What are some recurring negative thoughts you have about yourself? Where did they come from? How can you change these thoughts?

your creative
path enriches
you as you travel

Draw a map showing where you are and where you want to be. What obstacles are in your way? Where can you go and who can you visit to get help along your journey?

your relationship with time can be REDEFINED

If you could go back in time and change three decisions you made, what would they be? How can you use that knowledge in the future?

RISK LIVING OUT
your beautiful
dreams

Do you have a dream you think is silly or unrealistic?
Write about it, then share it with a trusted friend!

Know what you want.

Keep your eyes open.

No one can hit their target with closed eyes.

Write about a goal you would like to achieve.
Are there smaller goals you can tackle to achieve a larger goal?

we are
spinning
LIKE
Mad
confetti

Do you feel yourself pulled in a million different directions? What can you do to simplify your life so you can focus on what matters most?

Fill in each heart with something you're grateful for.
List them all at once or add one each day.

Wherever you
Shine your light
HAPPINESS GROWS.

Write down five ways you could make another person happy today.

What do you find yourself doing when you should
be doing something else?

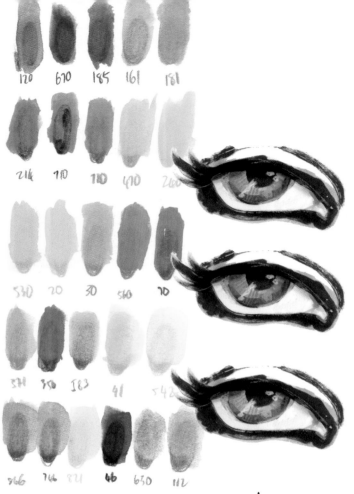

120 670 185 161 181

216 710 710 470 260

530 20 30 560 70

571 350 183 41 542

866 746 821 46 650 112

when they told me "NO"
I thought "for you maybe,
but not for me."
CYNDI LAUPER

Write about a time when you were told no to something you wanted to do, but you did it anyway. What were the results? Would you do it again?

every MOMENT
of searching
is a moment
of ENCOUNTER.

PAULO COELHO

If you could meet and talk to anyone, dead or alive, who would it be? What would you talk about?

Write a letter to your future self—ten, twenty, or thirty years in the future. Where do you see yourself? What dreams do you hope to have fulfilled?

Write about a chance you feel you missed or passed up.
If you had the chance again, would you take advantage of it?

Describe your ideal day or the best day you've ever had.
What elements of that day can you bring into your everyday life?

Throw me to the
Wolves,
and I will return
leading the PACK.

Write about a time you faced a tough situation and ended up stronger.

IN ANCIENT
times cats
were Worshipped
as GODS,
a fact they have
not forgotten.

What animal will you be reincarnated as in a future life and why?

Give me your
Magnificent
Protection

Which person in your life always has your back?
Who relies on you for support and protection?
How do these relationships enrich your life?

Sometimes you just have to
gather up your
Bravest Self
and head off into
the wild unknown.

Where would you most like to travel if money was no object?

*I don't think
there is ever
a wrong time
for a polka dot.*

MARC JACOBS

What is your trademark?
In your personal style, your artwork, your speech?

it feels
So GOOD
to tell the
TRUTH

FOXY BROWN

There's a difference between being truthful and imposing "your truth" on someone. How do you agree to disagree with someone when you don't quite see eye to eye?

unexpected
friendships
are the best ones.

Have you ever become friends with someone you didn't take to at first? What made you see them in a different light? How has their friendship enriched you?

if the ocean
can calm itself,
so can you.

We are both salt water
mixed with air.

Nayyirah WaHeeD

What upsets you or causes you stress? Take a deep breath.
How can you eliminate this stress from your life?

Protect
your
creativity.
BEFRIEND it.
It is your
strength in
Tough times.

Think of ten little ways you can be creative no matter how busy you are. (Arrange your kid's food in a picture, draw your grocery list instead of writing it, trace your self-portrait in the mirror with lipstick, invent a new dance move . . . anything goes!)

_____

_____

_____

_____

_____

_____

_____

_____

_____

Big dreams?

Elephantasize!

What is the biggest, most elephant-sized dream
you have ever dared to dream?

My best friend is the one who brings out the best in me.

HENRY FORD

Describe your best friend. How do they bring out the best in you?
How do you bring out the best in them?

Creativity
can look
DANGEROUS
to people who
MAY NOT HAVE FELT
its embrace
in a while...

What creative outlets do the people in your life enjoy and what encouragement and inspiration can you give to help them flourish?

Being glamorous is about Strength and Confidence. IT'S BLACK + WHITE, dramatic. You have to be strong.

CATHERINE ZETA-JONES

What are ten things that make you feel beautiful
and a little glamorous?

_____

_____

_____

_____

_____

_____

_____

_____

_____

_____

Keep the drama for your Art ♥

In what parts of your life do you feel you have too much drama?
How can you channel that energy into your creativity?

Art Supplies
are my very own
Creative
Menagerie

What do you collect? Why does it bring you joy?

Take time to
be a little
silly,
to color
OUTSIDE THE
lines + feel free!

What are some things you enjoyed doing as a child?
Is anything stopping you from doing them now?

you
always
have a
HOME.
...so fly
free...

Draw or describe your ideal home and sanctuary.
What about it makes it so comfortable and pleasant to be in?

Sugilite Genuine

Watching an artist at work is like seeing a Magician perform their magic.

(SO LET PEOPLE WATCH YOU CREATE!)

Do you have a hobby or other interest you don't share with people? Is there something people would be surprised to learn you're an expert at?

Pretend your name is a dictionary entry and write a definition of yourself. Are there multiple meanings?

What is most beautiful in your life?
Is it a physical object, a relationship?
Describe it or draw it!

Describe your superhero alter ego. Give her a name.
Who is your sidekick?

enjoy life's
Mystery

If you had a crystal ball, would you use it to see your future?

never stop
dreaming

Write down a strange or crazy dream you've had.
What do you think it means?

it's OK to stand out. A little flamboyancy makes life interesting.

Do you have a flamboyant side? Describe it. If not,
what can you do to stand out?

Scarlet Lake	Cad Red Purple	Perm Vermced
15		10
ure brill 1	Jaune brill 2	yellow ochre
2	23	2
greenish yellow	olive	T...t
	51	2
compose green 2	Compose geen 1	cobolt green
38	39	40
Manganese Blue Nova	Peacock	compose blue
		4
indigo	aynes	Neutral
54	55	56
Perm	Mineral	Mars

Make your own Rainbow

Invent your own rainbow! Make up new names for the colors. Summer rain? Kitten fur? New-mown grass? Come up with at least seven new hues.

Care AND Diligence bring LUCK.

T. fuller

Have you ever had a lucky break?
Was it really luck, or did your actions lead to it?

A love of color
gives zest !

How can you add more color to your life?

sway your
hips,
Dance
and
Dream

What song makes you get up and dance? Is it the music or the words that get you moving? What do you love about it?

Rainbowitis
is real.

I suffer from rainbowitis—the compulsion to collect and use art supplies. What is your self-diagnosis?

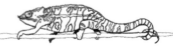